WORDS DANCE [15]
poetry mag

Winter 2013

WORDS DANCE PUBLISHING
WordsDance.com

EDITOR-IN-CHIEF
Amanda Oaks

CONTRIBUTING EDITORS
Rebecca Schumejda
John Dorsey
Jessica Dawson
Jason Neese

For more information, including submission guidelines, please visit:

WORDSDANCE.com

COVER ART BY

Rachelle Dyer

FEATURED ARTIST
photography by:

Nicola Taylor

POEMS BY:

- Meggie Royer • Susan Mahan •
- Rhiannon Thorne • Isla Anderson •
- Kristina Haynes • Dan Sicoli •
- Zeenie Sharif • Lisa Mangini •
- Dominique Lamontagne • Jay Sizemore •
- Claire Feild • Scott Silsbe •
- Linette Reeman • Mitchell Grabois •
- Marie Lascu • Amelia M. Garcia •
- Kathryn Roberts • Lydia Ford •
- Azra Tabassum • Aleathia Drehmer •
- Joseph Farley • T.M. Göttl •
- David Walker • Billi MacTighe •
- Danielle Donaldson • Scherezade Siobhan •
- Alex Sparks •

ADDITIONAL PHOTOGRAPHY BY:

- Koyna Tomar •

cover art by **RACHELLE DYER**

HAND IN HAND | *8x10 watercolor*

As a professional dancer and performer I am greatly inspired by movement and music. My artwork is motivated by my love and passion for dance. Painting acts as another outlet for me to reach a new audience and express myself artistically. I love the satisfaction of preserving a specific moment on stage or fleeting glance of a passionate performer. Visually I am always working to tell a story or share emotional experiences in a way that can be applied to anyone's situation, making art and an accessible experience for everyone!

RachellePaintings.com

featured artist
NICOLA TAYLOR

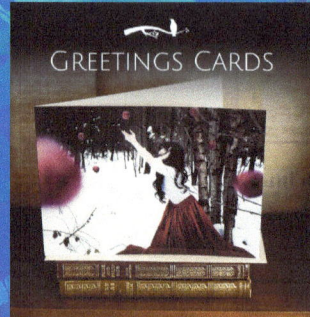

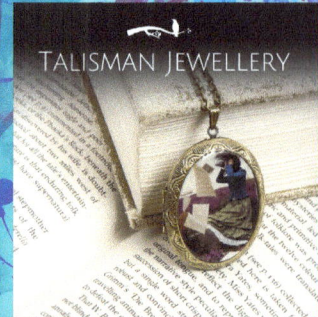

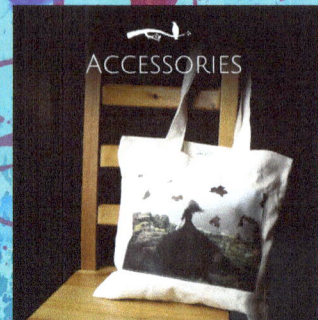

GREETINGS CARDS

TALISMAN JEWELLERY

PRINTS

ACCESSORIES

Nicola Taylor makes haunting, almost gothic images which she describes as a "still and silent storybook."

Each one is a labour of love, consisting of many images painstakingly stitched together in the computer to create a world that doesn't exist in reality.

Nicola believes that wild and desolate places inspire us to create stories more than any others, and growing up on the outskirts of the North Yorkshire Moors she experienced the influence a wild landscape can have over our creative consciousness, first as a child and now again as an adult.

NicolaTaylorPhotographer.com

No Light, No Light | **AMANDA OAKS**

Dear You,

Thank you.

Love,
Amanda

Midwinter | **NICOLA TAYLOR**

HITCHHIKER

This is what I know: my grandfather walked through seven miles of blizzard
to give my grandmother the wedding ring she would eventually lose in the fire.
The irony of weather is never lost on me now.
Sometimes love feels double-jointed for me because of all the years I spent
learning how to not flinch at my reflection in dinner spoons
while wishing to find someone else who would do the same only with forks.
Every autumn a flock of dead sparrows falls to the ground in my backyard
beneath the willow tree I once wished to be buried under,
the same tree I had childhood nightmares of growing into
until my bones fused with the roots and I became part of the dirt.
After the lost ring, my grandmother grieved the sparrows
instead of the absence on her finger and sometimes I wonder
if that's why holding her hands always felt like flight.
Those were the days when she would tell me stories
of how my grandfather fell for her after listening to her recite a poem
about how the spine married the back
and gave birth to the act of standing up straight after falling down.
It's no wonder no one in my family has a history of scoliosis.
And now every time I walk through a blizzard
it feels like falling in love.

– Meggie Royer

OPEN LETTER TO MY FIRST LOVE

I was young; I didn't know love like bloody handprints, bone marrow,
mouth like an oil spill. I was young; I didn't know where to put my tongue.
Somewhere on the quiet skin of my right shoulder,
there's still a hickey submerged from five years ago like Pangaea buried in the ocean.
In my dreams my father is sinking into piles of golden grain
six miles deep near two steady silos, but upon awakening
I find him sinking into the bed instead, telling me that's what falling in love feels like.
But you, you taught me that falling in love feels like slicing the umbilical cord.
And someone tore it so hard that even though it's been years since we left one another,
you still feel like a missing limb.
I was young;
I didn't know that you'd love me down to the bone,
down to the core, down to the roof of my mouth.
If someone dissected my belly five thousand years
after my death, they'd still find you inside of me
like petrified wood.

– Meggie Royer

SURVIVAL HYMN

Your grandmother said his entire kiss fit into her mouth
like a raisin soaked in olive oil, and they touched each other
with an urgency as if they'd been doused with lighter fluid
and had only seconds before they were lit on fire.
They visited the Holocaust museum together, of which
he was a survivor, and held hands while visiting the room
filled with piles of human hair. She said she had no idea
what he was thinking until her hand drifted down
to the back of his neck and rested there,
and his breath hitched like a static interruption
on the phone line. The first time they made love,
the sheets smelled like loss for days after,
and they took a picture of the bloodstain
to hang beneath a magnet on the fridge.
Your grandmother said that he kissed her thighs
as gently as if an entire city rested between them,
mourning the loss of his family in the flames
as she made sounds for which language has no words.

– Meggie Royer

COAT CHECK ROOM
New Year's Eve

I'm babysitting furs tonight.
I hang forty-two in all,
side by side by side
on polished wooden hangers.

Luxuriant and well-bred,
they are a docile assemblage

until their owners
leave the room.

I sit in the shadows and watch
as a mink rubs elbows with a beaver
and a raccoon cavorts with a fox.
A rabbit whispers secrets
at the collar of an ermine.

A stately sable skitters off in a huff
at the slight indiscretion of a seal:
a minor disturbance
in the peaceable kingdom.

Near midnight,
the rabbits rally the rest in a conga line,
and they swivel round and round the rack
to toast the New Year.

– Susan Mahan

TEETH

I do not have teeth like a movie star
they hang like bats,
clinging to the roof of my mouth, or
stalactites; they are utilitarian devices,
Swiss army knives and bullets,
a wrench when needed.

I flash them like breasts, their skin yellowed
with coffee and wine and smokey ventilation,
I weave them through conversation,
decking little battle rams
then close them like battlements; They are obscene,
and sometimes I use them
like little wasted dreams.

I will win no elections;
they do not sit like a politician, but they lie,
promises and promiscuity and salty nights,
they beg for the brush
and then the wisp of someone's skin
like a warm-blooded thing.

Already I can tell
they will not all make it out alive, my mercenary bones,
they are beginning to wear like rocks
from the saliva roll of my tongue
and the constant pressure
of verbs.

– Rhiannon Thorne

Fallen | **NICOLA TAYLOR**

NECTAR

The first she knew of her nectar
was that it could feed a swarm.

When she was seven,
the man with the tie who bought apple pie
from her mother's pastry shop

told her she was sweet
and walked her home across the street
whilst her mother cut fruit in the kitchen

and because he was a regular
and knew her mother well
and always praised her apple pies
as the 'sweetest ones in town',

she didn't know his hunger
wanted more than she could sell,

so let him take her daughter home
whilst she rolled income out of dough
in the kitchen of her pastry shop.

The first she knew of hunger
was that it loved like a swarm.

She was seven
when the man with stubble-jaw
did so much more than walk her home;

he closed the door
and took her like an apple core
from the ripeness of its fruit

and she could feel his stubble
loving her like stings; his body-swarm
and she was warm beneath his hands

like the bruised and pitted fruit
that her mother wouldn't use
unless the fresh was something
she could not afford.

The first she knew of apples
was the man who made her one
when he promised he would only
walk her home;

the hungry swarm
that undertook a human form
and stole the fruit from her mother's
precious kitchen.

– Isla Anderson

A LETTER TO MY TWIN

You were the ceiling that collapsed
from the scaffold of our mother's womb;

powder in the brickwork
where there should have been cement.

Did you know that I was coming?
think there wasn't room for two
in the plot between her hips?

Did you hear my heartbeat drumming
and offer up the spotlight
that shone out between her lips?

Wet paint, open wound-
shall I call you sister?:

I've never known
how to walk the red carpet
you painted for me;

how to wear the silk
of a second chance—

how could I sing
to the midwife's applause
as she slapped

my two foot soles
instead of our four?

Little loss, looking glass,
my god: the ruptured lung:

you taught me to pray
to an empty space
and call it my religion.

— Isla Anderson

VELVET

for the wife of a tuberculosis patient

there is luxury, and luxury
for I have known the velvet of your lungs
like a lover's darkened room;

swathed myself, naked,
in the satin of your voice

and slept beneath the sheets
of your every inhalation:
those crimson folds; that drapery

now wet and worn
from the years we've spent
shawled in each other's breathing;

the perfume of our evening
shall not linger on your sheets

but is gasped away
by the slow decay
that consummates our bed;
stains the linen red--

there's no white flag to wave
but the frayed and bloody thread
that's unraveling your chest

as we lie here in silence, tending
to the moths that feed on velvet--

that luxury; that luxury.

– Isla Anderson

The Weaker Side | **NICOLA TAYLOR**

Evensong | NICOLA TAYLOR

I HAVE BEEN GROWING MY HAIR OUT SINCE I WAS FIFTEEN

I have been growing my hair out since I was fifteen
and this is the most interesting thing about me. It's not
an easy thing, accepting that the boys I love go home
to other people at the end of the day. Yet the world
continues to turn. I play my music loudly and do not
apologize for it. Maybe I should tell you that I've been
hiding love affairs in shoe boxes that I stash beneath
my bed. At the hair salon the other day, when the
stylist was trimming my split ends, I decided that I
never want to get married. I'm too sentimental for the
21st century and cry over modern things, like plumbing
and airports and espresso machines. I will have more
boyfriends and I know this. I do not apologize for it.
Sometimes I am really afraid of the knife in my hands
as I chop up onions and potatoes and peppers. I say
change and expect it to happen instantly. I lose the same
things, repeatedly, over and over again. An untwinned
earring. Hair ties. Mechanical pencils. A secret is:
I'll love you. Even when I don't.

– *Kristina Haynes*

DIRTY HOTEL ROOM BLUES

It is easy to get away when you need to.
There are planes and trains and buses. There are maps.
There are hotel rooms. I set down my suitcase

and fumble for the light switch, root around in the mini bar
until I find a bottle of whiskey. It's not my drink of choice,
but it will dull the humming in my brain,

the stark image of him fucking a stranger over the sink
in the kitchen, the look on his face when he saw me.
I stand in front of the long mirror in the bathroom,

heavy-lidded from the alcohol, and peel my opaque tights
from my thighs. Then down my knees. My calves are next,
and I am hating this, hating him, because he loved my legs,
loved to do this, undress me, take me out of my work

clothes and lick my skin until I'm shivering.
After lying down, I think vaguely of black lights and
what they say about hotel beds and bodily fluids.

I rub a pillow against my breasts, fake a moan to hear
what it sounds like and miss him so fucking much
that I can't breathe. I can only imagine how sad I look.

In the morning I vomit twice and fold my hair into itself
to see how I'd look with the mess of it shorn off, chin-length--
all of it gone save for new growth. Instead I brush it out

and put it up. Mourn the shallowness of my collarbones,
the window that is painted shut. I pick up the bobby pins
and start over.

– Kristina Haynes

GODFATHER

today
that door could be on an elusive asteroid
but it's still exactly 47 paces from
my parents' front porch
since the day i counted them
the boring summer
when i was nine
and had my arm entombed in plaster

now on this visit as a young man
just eighteen
i watch people entering and exiting
fearful this parade will be a long slow walk
my stadium face nearly breaking

having no idea
i brought you chocolates
a bottle of red
what's the harm now

your warm and open greeting
invented smile
in spite of swellings
and you joked and
lent me a laughter
i would never return

you'd grimace mid-sentence
tap the morphine pump
i wanted to be so much like you

later when you told me of endless discomfort
even seated
your backside felt as if each pocket
contained two huge wallets
i could only squeeze your hand
and then let go

i am powerless, godfather
learning
infinity has bounds

– Dan Sicoli

SILHOUETTE
for M

My dear, beautiful friend
you wear sand dollars for eyes
and pebbled combs for teeth.

I meet you, a fevered bundle of
blue-ribbon coal, beneath the gravity
of our tumbled shadows.
I feel how strong the weakness is
when our heads touch;
I must crawl my tired fingers
into the cracks of your wrist
to ensure you still remember
how to maintain a pulse.

I feel how boldly your darkness
spits. A bad performance poet
hurling blindness instead of words,
it tells you to walk forward
while it plucks the entire spectrum
of light from the holes in your corneas.
It calls you a choking frailty
for wanting to use a cane,
for needing landmarks
to find your way to something
you can call home.

You cry out loud so silently,
unsure if the broken mirrors
under your tongue are supposed to be there,
if you should always taste
the liquid metal of blood
in your swallow.
The crevices of your mind have claws,
tiny crabs gnawing through
the wires that hold up your lights.

Brightness splashes from your lips
when you speak,
shattered flashlights that have
no choice but to eternally shine.
You only see the bruised plastic,
the dead wires, the crushed face —
you see no reason to use flashlights
when they are broken.

And I am sorry.
Sorry I cannot guide you
out of the evil prism maze,
sorry there are so many voices
that you cannot recognize
your own,
sorry there are too many reflections
and all of them look like monsters.

But you re-gift your pain more beautifully
than anyone I have ever seen
and I believe in calling things what they are
but I cannot say what I see in your eyes
is emptiness.

So let me tell you stories
you've always thought yourself too scarred
to hear and let me show you
how my lies keep growing,
but so does my love.
Let me remind you that we
are not empty.

— Zeenie Sharif

PAINTED FIRE, I.

We considered going out, not wanting cabin fever, not wanting to go stir crazy, after a day cooped up in air conditioning, or waste a day when Paul didn't have to tend to patients, a rare holiday not reserved for the hospital. He talked me into a drive through the countryside, one way to spend time for a while: pass under the shadow of silos, watch the fireworks from behind the windshield, kiss in the dark off rural route one-twenty-nine. Independence Day meant making ourselves younger, pretzeled in the front seat, behind the blind spot of anonymous barns, pretending we were too young to have our own place with privacy, younger than when we even knew each other.

– Lisa Mangini

A HAIKU FOR EACH RELATIONSHIP I'VE EVER HAD

1. It turns out I was
not quite enough and you soon
found someone who was.

2. This haiku is of
a much longer length than our
relationship was.

3. We met through friends but
that was the only thing that
we had in common.

4. I thought you loved me,
but you were angry when I
didn't want to fuck.

5. In the end, it turned
out that you loved your sadness
more than you loved me.

6. Your hands felt foreign
on my skin. you were only
a tourist in me.

7. You proved that getting
high was your way of coping
with feeling so low.

8. Your beard on my thighs
confirmed my 'daddy issues'
(I'm sorry for that)

9. You are beautiful.
I watch you move and I can't
think straight. Ironic.

— Dominique Lamontagne

REFLECTION IN THE GRASS

Yard work leads to sunburn, but is necessary for the appearance of sophistication to passing drivers. A backwards hat soaks up the sweat from my brow, my long hair swept in stringy strands across my face and neck. Pulling weeds. Fighting an uphill push against this downhill stampede of tangled roots and stems displacing the homogeny of redwood chips. The neighbor's shrubs started out the day less flat. It seems a silent competition is always engaged here. Whose flowers have bloomed. Who's let their monkey grass go untended.

★

The mailbox is set at an odd tilt. A man could go crazy thinking of all the ways his life doesn't fit into right angles. Driving home, I noticed a decent recliner set by the curb. I wanted it, but had no way to drag it back with me. An hour later, I saw the chair in the bed of a red truck, and I hoped it was infested with bedbugs or fleas. Sometimes life is like playing roulette, one chamber loaded with confetti.

★

The yard is mowed, edges trimmed. My back feels like a fresh tattoo. They say you shouldn't write near open windows. But from here, I have seen children pedaling their bikes through the heat. I've noticed the tiny smears left behind by cats' noses. I've seen the sky dim into that purplish-pink, framed by shadows of tree tops and the stark outlines of houses. While the ice has melted in the glass of bourbon beside me, I've felt serene in that tired ache one can only feel after finishing something. There is comfort in knowing the universe is capable of bending, but most of the time, it won't.

– Jay Sizemore

ROVING

The rolls of sand lead us to a
transient green, the contents
of this hole wet with leaves
dancing above grit that is
grazing. We cup our hands
before reaching for what we
think will be warm water
to soothe our cuts from
our constantly moving
from one significant place
to an insignificant one and
vice-versa. The feel of
clarity emerges as we wash
our hands in the best water
we can find.

– Claire Feild

ONE NIGHT AT DUKE'S

Every passing day means one or two lost memories.
Duke's Bar wasn't much to talk about really, but I
can remember a good night there, scouring the juke
trying to find us some greasy hits, all hunched over
next to the life-size John Wayne cardboard stand-up.

The beer was cheap and cold and the tables weren't
too wobbly. I can't remember what we talked about
at all, Kris. I can remember being drunk enough to
approach a girl I found sexy, though once I started
talking with her I realized that I had nothing to say.

Instead I got her some free cigarettes and retreated
back to my beer. So Duke's Bar is long gone now,
replaced by two chain burrito shops and a sub place.
That girl is long gone too. But I do still get postcards
on occasion from the Marlboro Cigarette Company.

– *Scott Silsbe*

HOW TO GET OVER A GIRL WITH DESERT EYES

step one: try to coax her back—
make yourself as hollow
as birdcages, as brittle as branches,
tell her, "look, there's room
in here—i've cleared it out for you."
but she's scared of birds, hates
leaves rustling under the humid sun
of your heart (they remind her of
your hair), so she stays away.

step two: talk to new people—
let her boyfriend kiss you/break
the three of you in pieces/throw out your
instruction manual, because he didn't have time
to organize his heart (play match-maker; stitch
them back together—never forget how his lips tasted—
and steal him when they finally disband).

step three: hate yourself—

(this is easy)

step four: hate her—

(this is harder)

step five: go shopping—
you accidentally fall in love, and your new
sweetheart's lighthouse tongue does wonders for
your shipwrecked heart. you tell her about
this desert-eyed girl, this scapegoat/sugar-coat
back-and-forth that's been wearing down the rigging
under your bones, and your darling unfurls
the treasure map of your skin; the x's on her
fingers mark every place she takes you to, every
constellation-brimming promise in her smile.
your new lover has ocean eyes and laughs like
birds, sings like leaves (you fall in love as much as
you did before, but these times only with her).

step six: forget—
she stops answering your calls;
you take a hint and tell her you'll still wake up praying
to the universe that you don't trip over her obituary;
you call her the pet name, end with "goodbye."

step seven: remember—
(but only the good things)
you start writing poetry about her
again, but very slowly, like a child
taking first steps, or blindness
teaching itself how to play piano.

– Linette Reeman

Abstractions | **KOYNA TOMAR**

Fall | **KOYNA TOMAR**

Murakami | **KOYNA TOMAR**

SIGN

Sign painter in our town—
not too smart
Did he drop out
or just never go?

but gentle-natured
a smile on his weathered face,
people hire him
when they need letters in the air

He wanted to do tattoos
but he was terrible
and that shit's permanent

Hospital administrator
came out one overcast day
and said:
What's that?

"Surgery Entrance"
said the sign painter
but he'd spelled it Sugary
Sweet, said the administrator

Head of the Board said:
We can't live with this
You gotta hire someone else

But business improved
People stopped going to the big hospital
across the county
and stayed home to get cut

They liked thinking it was sugary
even though
they knew it wasn't

— Mitchell Grabois

POACHERS HAVE KILLED ALL RHINOS IN MOZAMBIQUE PARK

If skin came off in full at the tug of
what bloomed in me that week,
I could have painted walls with a touch,

braid my hair and coo to soften me,
all of these things have passed and do pass,
somersault as children to flip your belly
which aches and aches and aches,

palm shadows my eyes in the boiling sun,
superstition cooks its books and marvels
at what can be taken without reserve,

for the all healing answer to what ails you,
the quiet I wish for you should bury you
standing not in honor but to flame,

had the last one stood in the shade?

– Marie Lascu

THE BUBONIC PLAGUE SPEAKS TO HIS THERAPIST

after Desireé Dallagiacomo

I need to know someone can fix me.
It's really hard living like this, you know.
I was in love.
And I knew it would hurt.
It always does, right?
It's always the open mouth of a mass grave.

She was a dancer when no one was watching.
Humans have funny ways of dealing with grief.
Her family made bonfires
behind their rural home
hoping to hide in the smoke.
That's exactly how I found her.
That trail of embers.
The first time I saw her,
she was dancing,
her untainted flesh a smear of white,
the color of flames licking her orange.
She was more alive than anything I had ever seen.

The night I finally approached her,
she stopped cold in the middle of a doorway.
When she saw me she begged for others.
Stab wound.
Animal attack.
Swift poison.
Anyone but me.
My love is a sickness.
A bucket full of dirty water.
Everyone's holding their breath around here.
Even you wear that mask
and carry those damned herbs.
I know I'm awful.
I don't need to be reminded.
But Death.

Death has always been a greedy bastard.
He's always taking.
It didn't really matter before,
but I wanted so badly for her to want me.
Instead, I had to leave a bouquet of flowers on her doorstep
the morning she died.
It was the only gift I was able to give her.

My love is not a gift.
It's something I don't know how to do without flinching
or turning the most tender things to bursting boils
then dust.
I'm so tired of being lonely,
but I'm more afraid of this:
There's nothing that mortality won't touch.
I loved her.
I would've ripped that feeling right out of me
if I knew where to find it.
I don't want this to happen again.

Some say I was born in the swollen belly of a ship at sea
and then catapulted over siege walls
until I was old enough to find my feet.
My entire life has been a journey toward her ending.
Some days love feels like an unbreakable commitment.
Tell me, please tell me
there's a way to get out of this.

– Amelia M. Garcia

THE ALCOHOLIC CONSIDERS ANOTHER ROUND

I don't know much, but I do know this:
There are things you can say
to a half-empty bottle
that you can't say to a person.

When I walk into this bar
there's already a beer waiting for me.
Beer is my favorite drinking partner.
It doesn't ask questions.
It's always ready for another round.
It reminds me alcoholism runs in my veins,
and if I cut myself open
I wouldn't find even four days sober.

There's a woman at the end of the bar
trying to flirt her way into a cocktail.
She looks just like my mother.
Beer says, "Your mother is a busted lighthouse
that's no good at direction.
She's the crooked compass
on the map of your homeland."
Beer is correct.
And I come here to prove her right.
I am worth forgetting.

Beer doesn't like when I get sad.
It tells me a story about cats.
But once, while drunk and on the verge of tears,
I explained to my now ex-girlfriend that
one side of my family tree has low hanging branches
weighed down by the memory of alcohol abuse.

The other side sees things that aren't actually there.
I am a convergence of battered roots.

And my grandmother told me she doesn't drink

because she's scared to end up like her father,
a man I've never known.
She said a life of utter sobriety was a better choice
than whatever monster she feels she will become.

Beer tells me to ignore these stories,
says family history is what you make of it,
like the way I've rewritten the word home
to be nothing more than the cracked vinyl of a bar stool.

But you haven't seen the family photos, Beer.
I look just like my grandmother's fear.

– Amelia M. Garcia

FIRST LOVE

My ex-husband used to break bottles
with his palm, at parties. Drink down
the beer, then add back in an inch of water,
or maybe two--my memory, for the first
time, more focused on the act
than the number. Then, pulled-back
hand smashed flat to bottle, the bottom
breaking apart, shattering down
and skittering across the patio.
They all tried it, the macho men
we married, empty displays of power
that we already knew in private
but pretended to be proud of in public.
I wonder if he's shown his new wife the trick,
let her stand there, uncomfortably pretending
to admire a hand that only knows
purpose in destruction.

- Kathryn Roberts

UNCHARTED TERRITORY

My body is a paper map,
lined with unknown street names
and ghost towns,
dotted with pushpins
for everywhere I wish you'd be;
my hipbones are mountains,
curved and vacant
like empty parentheses,
waiting for the compass needles
of your fingers
to tell me where to go.
My body is a paper map
and I am just a
hopeless wanderer.

– Lydia Ford

A Soul that Sees Beauty | **NICOLA TAYLOR**

QUESTIONS I WILL ASK MY DAUGHTER WHEN SHE COMES HOME CRYING

Why are your hands wet,
have you been trying to hold the rain again?

Did you cup your palms against the inner lining of the sky
and grasp at the edges so you could wrap it around you
like a blanket? Did the clouds turn their back?

Did they shake the cold all over you?
Did it seep into your bones? Is your bird heart
trembling inside your body?

Don't you realise that it's impossible to gather all the hurt
you have inside of you in the shallow of your two small palms?

Here, give it to me, let me carry it for you.
Don't blink back your tears, don't you know
that sometimes it is good to hurt?

That sometimes saltwater is healing, that your face
needs to learn the difference between tears and thunderstorms?

And even the sea is not always your friend
but you have to let yourself lie in it long enough
that you can find the strength to get back up.
And baby, do you want to use blankets or your own arms
to fix yourself into shape again?

Don't let them tell you that you don't have the strength
to ease yourself into gentleness again
and don't you know that there's a difference between
being soft and being weak and you are not weak.
Did you hear about the woman who screamed your name hoarse
but held you like you were rose petals at the same time?

This is the kind of love you were forged from, the gasping
breathing kind of love so you can pound your fists against your chest
or rip yourself open for strangers either way
you'll never be anything less than rock hard.

So let me tell you it is okay to cry and leak sadness until there are puddles
brimming at your feet,
did you hear about the boy who slept in the rain
so he could turn himself inside out and be okay again?

Did you see the way he looked when he came home, with his eyes
falling down his face and his fingers like dates
his smile was the brightest I've seen and haven't you heard
that there is something about water that will make you new again?

- Azra Tabassum

FOR HOWEVER LONG THAT MIGHT BE

We awake in the early afternoon
when the last evidence
of morning's existence
creeps through the covered windows.

The damp breeze lifts the blinds
and taps them against the sill.

He rolls halfway over,
back still facing me
and tells me he dreamed
I sent him back to California
because of his allergies;
he says I hand delivered him
to the airport to be sure
he was gone.

There couldn't be anything further
from the truth of reality
but I suppose this is what dreaming
is for, expelling fears
and bridging disconnects.

We sit up against the pillows
the room filled with the smell
of sleep until he lifts the blinds
and lets in the spring.

The light rain pools water in the road
and the tires of cars make a familiar
sound as they move through them—
a sound so comforting
I can never seem to describe it.

I finish a book about grief
listening to these sounds
mixed with his breathing

and the smell of his skin
drifting on the air through the screen.

These moments I have taken for granted
believing they will always be here
when I want them, but I know how life works,
how it renders down the fat
and leaves us with little left to taste.

I want to tell him this,
want to whisper in his ear
how lucky I am to know him
for however long that might be,

but the moment passes
and the domestic nature of our day
begins, something no less wonderful,
but distracting. It would leave the sentiment
out of place and he'd worry I was sad,
so I just smile as he leaves the room,
still happy to know him, for however
long that is, in secret.

– Aleathia Drehmer

LUCK

My wife was obsessed with luck.
Anything that went wrong in life
was due to bad luck.
There was no need
for self examination
or descent into guilt or shame.

The house was decorated
with bagua mirrors
to keep away bad energy;
red tasseled symbols
of good fortune;
Chinese scrolls and characters
for luck and wealth;
statues of merciful GuanYin.

With all these peripheral devices
you would think the demon winds
would not have a chance
of getting into our home,
but they still did.

Maybe there were no symbols
at her office or the school
where she went to study opera,
or the restaurants where she ate
and drank beer and wine
with smiling men.

Or maybe I have this all wrong.
Maybe those romances
were good luck for her.
Maybe the bad luck
had gotten into the house
before she put up her magic.
Maybe the bad luck was me,
a mistaken choice in marriage.

Maybe. There is always maybe.
There is always
"If things had been different."
There is always
"If I could do things over."
Maybe. Maybe it does not matter.
Maybe it was all just luck after all.

I wish her good luck now.
I wish me the same.
There is enough hurt to go around.
I will take this table with me.
I will take two chairs.
I will take my books.
I will take my memories,
Good and bad.

She can keep the rest,
including all the luck symbols.
Clearly they always
belonged to her anyway.

– Joseph Farley

THE BASTARDS

Who are these bastards
that rule the world?

What rocks do they
breed under?

Where do they get
their forked tongues
that spit flame?

How do they open
their tight dirty fingers,

stained with blood
and gold

long enough
to point their guns
at our heads?

– Joseph Farley

Music for thosw who listen | NICOLA TAYLOR

Like Ghosts from an Enchanter Fleeing | **NICOLA TAYLOR**

PATRON OF THE IMPOSSIBLE

Your seraph wings were severed
from your blood-birthed body,
sealed in wax, and stored
under St. Peter's floorboards until
your heartspace-emptied return.
But don't surrender to your crumbly impatience—
Icarus fell as winged men always do,
but he didn't die—that is a lie-story
keeping winged creatures grounded.

Your list of prayer flags
looks like bleached surrenders.
The crumpled yellow bird
twitches in your chest
while the ravens circle,
shedding gold-black feathers
between your left and right ears.

Do not give in to the banjo-picking devil,
offering cool wine and river silt.
Do not take his hand,
shushing African violets through your
ram's horn veins.
Do not listen to the unhope ballads,
tracking muddy footprints through every nightmare's mane.

The Patron of the Impossible knows your intentions:
the pills, the knife, the closed door.
Patron of the Forgotten knows mistaken identities,
knows cold candles and penny-by-penny losses.
Patron of the Hopeless knows the
empty of the quiet bed.
Patron of Can't and Won't and No
knows the heatlamp desire-to-make—
to make jewelry, to make art, to make sweaters and jackets and crocheted scarves,
to make the grades, to make war, to make money,
to make dinner, to make peace, to make cookies,
to make music, to make love, to make gods,

to make angel medicine
that settles into the lowest point of your heels.

Patron of the Impossible knows,
weaving 747 contrails into nets
to break your fall. He sings a song rope,
casts into open fault fissures
and lassos the earth's burning belly to plant god–fire under every step you take,
burning you too hot, burning you too bright,
burning you to dream your lion dreams.

You are only light.
Every tree, every mosquito, every fungus, hair, dolphin,
every speck of mold, every dog and salmon and tobacco leaf and honeybee,
are only oddly-shaped light, light like supernovas
Morse coding "love" to your toes and fingertips,
light puzzles snapping into the borderless whole,
and any missing pieces leave a darkness void.
You are chosen by egg and bone and sun,
by the talon and the pottery shard.
You are chosen by the fractures in your lungs
and the Morpho butterfly's stained glass wing.
You are wrapped in catgut and drumheads,
and every time you move,
you play your song against the universe.
You are only one piece of light.
You are only the most important piece.

– T.M. Göttl

DR. BAYLOR'S CHILDHOOD

It would always be at night.

Later,
I would learn that
I never achieved REM.

I would lie in my bed picking out creaks
and shadows

and stare in twilight. I never
fell fully asleep. My
father would swing
the door open and catch it before

it hit the wall on the
other side. He wanted
me to know he was there
but he didn't want
to offend his wife.

He wasn't cruel, after all.
Then he would pad over to my bed,
confident,

as if he was strolling
down a sidewalk
or meeting
a friend for coffee
and

he would peel my blankets off me –
my skin would hold
tight as if a Band-Aid were
being ripped off of it
and
he would plop in the bed
with me,

"I'm sure glad your mommy
let me stay the night, Jimmy.
Let's try not to make too
much noise tonight."
and I remember

how I just wanted to sleep.

– David Walker

ATTEMPTING TO REASON MY DIAGNOSIS

Describe *hurting*: The feel of closing
digits in a door, or the wedge
of the lazy susan built into the cabinets.
Define it without using *pain*: My swim
instructor, family friend, committing suicide
for owing money and getting drunk.
Or *loss*: My pony dying
while I was at school, fourth grade,
and never getting to say goodbye.
Or *physicality*: My right elbow
through the living room's french door
on the night of my tenth birthday.
Describe *soul-pain*: My best friend
found dead, hanging from a pipe
in his college dorm room.
Inner pain: The pain of being left
in an asylum at age fourteen,
for writing a note about depression.
Beyond the bone pain: My mother
not being able to look at me
after seeing how I mutilated
my wrists, my future. How
my father cried when everyone
else was silent, sitting in the
therapist's office at Pembroke.
Describe *mind-pain, brain-pain*:
When Kasey joined the Navy
and stopped talking to me
on my nineteenth birthday,
leaving her boyfriend to explain
how she hates me for what I've done.
And *what if I really am insane sort of pain*:
Like seeing shadows come to life,
creating monsters that I know
aren't there because it makes me feel
something other than the numb
of existing alone. Tell me
what it's like to *hurt*.

The doctors say I shouldn't know.

– Billi MacTighe

Raven's Song | NICOLA TAYLOR

WOMEN

I've had a sticky note on my bathroom mirror for over a month
"Call Grandma" in black marker
And once I do, I know that she'll sound out of breath
From running to the small table and chair in the hallway
Where the old corded phone still sits.
And she tells me about
Indian summer, you too?
Are you healthy? Sleeping well?
Did you get my card?
He's great. It's all great. The doctor says he'd doing fine.
I'm retiring again. I have a terrible disease.
She pauses to make my throat swell close.
It's called TMB—Too Many Birthdays!
She laughs with a start. And my brain starts chugging along again
So I can laugh with her.
How's your father?
She clucks her tongue.
Her oldest son, her constant disappointment,
The judgment runs down in the Irish Catholic blood
But she'll forgive him and herself come Saturday morning confession.
Glad you're doing well, honey. I can feel her weathered smile
and weak armed hugs in her voice.
When I hang up much too quickly, I remember when
I sat at her kitchen table
And asked her, my face was still smooth with my earnest,
What kind of woman should I be?
As I drug the doily under the salt and pepper shaker between
my bitten fingernails.
She put down her tea and closed her mouth tightly.
It's not about the woman you ought to be. But the woman you already are.
She patted my arm as she went to stir the dinner on the stove.

– Danielle Donaldson

REUNION

Sticky blue cotton candy
Stuck in the ruts of your teeth
I can taste it melting on your lips
Years after that summer was gone
Those beach sunburns have aged your eyes
And dulled your lights
But with my fingertips
Under your thin shirt
I can still feel the universe
Brewing in your chest

– *Danielle Donaldson*

Washed Away | **NICOLA TAYLOR**

BEFORE PASHTO

We were drunk on Fellini
and the clouds had crumpled cliff-side
as if a papier mâché umbrella.
My body : strapped to the last
slivers of gravity falling under
yours like a bough of bluebells
tendered by novice snow.
There were fireworks migrating
to the jagged depths of our pupils.
Our hours were a scandal of shrunken gasps
because my skin had run out of similes
to describe the urgent pilgrimage
of your hands to my heart, my whole
-ness swallowed by this small mouth of mercy
that opened beneath the black marrow
of a funeral shaped night. We were
meager and heady : a catharsis in Kabul.
Our insides stammered as though torn
dictionaries; we made love
curled like saw-toothed taproots and
outside the wind honed its falsetto
on the cut lip of a broken window.
Inside, a country collapsed dimly
into a fragile whisper.

— Scherezade Siobhan

PALINDROME

Love, how long will you let him
treat your body
like a holocaust?
He found you flickering
on a pearled page : a cathedral
of swarovski words lit in grace
You were
disobedient like Free Verse.
subterranean like a haiku.
sublime like a Sonnet.
Now your poems die
in the inkwell of a stilled throat
Your voice has turned into a ballad
gone black.

You carry a scar tissue for a heart.
The years in your palms turning to
an alphabet of bruises tapped into the skin of
your soul like an invisible morse code.
You are an architecture of antithesis.
–curate and corrupt.
–ageless and abrupt.
How did you let him
turn your body into the violence
of crumbled chalk dotting the
inner city pavements?

Your body was Time unveiled.
Now it lies inert as fallen seconds
: an exhausted molotov cocktail.
To give him shelter,
you became a perpetual homelessness
a matryoshka doll draped in 3 kinds of sadness
when unfastened from grasp of his unforgiving hands.
You used to be the brunette hair of horizon
parted across unmeasured distances
by a skein of blackbirds.

Now, you are bare; narrow
a vagabond feather
weather-beaten in the vise of a line storm.

How neatly you tucked all the ghosts
under the flute of your wrists
soaked your songs in saffron
threw seasalt across all the circles
the pain drew inside your belly
every time he left your insides
capsized : a purblind catamaran.

This hunger you birthed is a nomad
& many blurred rivers float
inside the mirage of desire.
& you see, absence is rust;
the dullest red stammering its fullness
against the iron cage of your ribs.

As heartbeats as hummingbird
blue-dusk; as breath as brocade
of afghan verse; as skin as the
sycamore starved by light.

Did no one tell you that
love is a palindrome?
It should read the same both ways
& if his mouth is lessened by the full nuance
of your name; you must find another tongue
to treasure the whole

language that
You were
written in.

– Scherezade Siobhan

GET WELL SOON AND OTHER HOMEMADE GREETING CARDS

There are entire rooms in the hospital of my body
I have not slept in since you left me.
There are sick white hallways inside of me,
that I still look for you in.

When you told me you were sick,
I laughed like a junior high,
like my mouth was a middle school dance.
I laughed like a locker room,
like a wet towel keeps the smoke in.
There is nothing I can say to make you better.

You look so beautiful in baby blue.
How dare you look so damn ravishing in a cotton hospital gown?
The doctors called you the prettiest cadaver they'd ever seen.
I called you "love me with the lights on"
swore you'd never have to kiss the dark from my face.
On my good days, I'm still changing light bulbs.

When you told me you were sick,
I waited for the punchline,
for the creak in your voice and
the crack in your smile.
Hoped to God you'd suck the words back in.

I threw my hand into a floor length mirror,
threw my Bible off the Huntington Beach pier.
The doctors called you a walking miracle,
said I should be thankful for the weeks you fought for.

When you finally stopped calling it sick and
admitted you were dying,
I kissed the words from your mouth,
held you in like the baby blue.

On my bad days, I still write you greeting cards.
Sometimes "Get Well Soon" is the easiest way to say
Goodbye.

— Alex Sparks

SLEEPING THROUGH PLUM SEASON

Bite through your hardest dark.
Hold the whole world in your mouth
like a ripe plum. Spit out
nothing but light.
Keep the seeds under your tongue.
Pray for someone with enough dark
to kiss you back.
Pray for the ghost of a gardener;
a white sheet and dirty fingernails.

– Alex Sparks

Listen to the Colour of Your Dreams | **NICOLA TAYLOR**

BIOS

Meggie Royer is a writer and photographer from Iowa who currently lives in St. Paul, Minnesota. Her poetry and prose touch on healing and recovery through love. Her work has been published in Lost Freedom Magazine, Winter Tangerine Review, Words Dance Magazine, and more. In March 2013, her writing portfolio won a National Silver Medal in the 2013 Scholastic Art & Writing Awards, and her poetry collection won a National Gold Medal. Poetry will always be her compass for navigating the rough, stormy seas of life. writingsforwinter.tumblr.com

Susan Mahan has been writing poetry since her husband died in 1997. She is a frequent reader at poetry venues and has written four chap books. She joined the editorial staff of The South Boston Literary Gazette in 2002. She has been published in a number of journals and anthologies, including Words Dance #14.

Rhiannon Thorne grew up in Santa Rosa, CA, but currently resides in Phoenix, Arizona. Her work has appeared/is forthcoming most recently in Foundling Review, Midwest Quarterly, and The Doctor TJ Eckleburg Review. When she's not busy with a book or a pen, she spends her time daydreaming about becoming a home brewer. Admittedly, this usually involves sampling a microbrew (or two). She also co-edits the online publication cahoodaloodaling with fellow poet-in-arms, Kate Hammerich, and may be reached at rhiannonthorne.com.

Isla Anderson was born in Surrey and lives and writes as a student just outside of London. Her poetry has been published in The Yeah Write! Review, Linden Avenue and the Adroit Journal amongst others, and she was commended in the Foyle Young Poets of the Year award 2013. When she isn't writing, she spends her time painting, sleeping and observing strangers in public places.

BIOS

Kristina Haynes is 22 years old currently residing in the suburbs of Pennsylvania. After graduating from her current school, she hopes to pursue a Bachelor's Degree in Musical Theatre in New York City. Her work has been featured in several literature magazines including Freckled and The Laconic and she has recently published a chapbook of poetry, *It Looked a Lot Like Love* through Where Are You Press this past November.

Dan Sicoli writes about hope and the fallout that comes from offering it up. He is the author of two poetry chapbooks from Pudding House Publications (Columbus, Ohio), *Pagan Supper* and *the allegories*. In addition to co-founding and co-editing the literary press and magazine Slipstream, his work has appeared in numerous litmags, e-zines, anthologies, and poetry audio recordings. Currently, he can be found in local dives, saloons and barrelhouses banging on an old Gibson 335 as a rhythm guitarist with an area rock'n'roll band.

Zeenie Sharif is a nineteen-year-old girl from New Jersey. She writes to feel the world simultaneously open up and fall away, to tell her own stories and the stories of others. When she isn't writing, she's trying ridiculous ice cream flavors, creating art, and meeting new people.

Lisa Mangini holds an MFA from Southern Connecticut State University. Her poetry collection, "Bird Watching at the End of the World," is forthcoming from Cherry Grove in 2014. She is the winner of the 2011 Connecticut Poetry Prize, and her work can be found in Weave, Stone Highway Review, Louisiana Literature, and others. She is the founding editor of Paper Nautilus, and teaches English composition and creative writing at handful of colleges across Connecticut. You can find reviews, event dates, and contact her at: facebook.com/lisa.mangini.mfa

BIOS

My name is **Dominique Lamontagne**. I'm unruly, I don't like capital letters, and I really do love oxford commas. I'm aware things don't always work out the way people intend them to, so all I cling to is my poetry, and I hope one day it pays my rent. facebook.com/dominiquelamontagnewriting

Jay Sizemore is Associate Poetry Editor for Mojave River Review. He writes poetry and short fiction that offends his family. He is way behind on reading the classics. His work has appeared in places like Ayris, Red River Review, DASH, and Spry. His poem "My Despair Trivialized" was nominated for Best of the Net 2013 by Cease, Cows. He currently lives in Nashville, TN, home of the death of modern music. facebook.com/poetJay

Claire T. Feild is an English composition instructor. She has had poems accepted for publication in numerous journals & her second collection of poetry. *Southern Aunts, The 1950s*, has just been published (Summer 2013). An Origami chapbook is in press & her first poetry book is *Mississippi Delta Women in Prism*.

Scott Silsbe was born in Detroit. He now lives in Pittsburgh, where he sells books, makes music, and writes. His poems have recently appeared in The Chariton Review, Nerve Cowboy, and the Pittsburgh Post-Gazette. He is the author of *Unattended Fire* (Six Gallery Press, 2012) and the forthcoming collection *The River Underneath the City* (Low Ghost, 2013).

BIOS

Linette Reeman is a high school senior who is no stranger to letting people poke around in her head, and invites them to do so through her writing. She has won multiple regional Scholastic writing awards, was published in the Fall 2012 Creative Communication anthology, and has recently begun performing as a spoken word poet. She lives in New Jersey with her family, her girlfriend, and her Star Trek paraphernalia. Her e-book *"SHUT UP!"* is available through Lulu.com.

Mitchell Krochmalnik Grabois was born in the Bronx and now splits his time between Denver and a one-hundred-and-twenty-year-old, one room schoolhouse in Riverton Township, Michigan. His short fiction and poems have appeared in hundreds of literary magazines in the U.S. and internationally. He has been nominated for the Pushcart Prize, most recently for his story "Purple Heart" published in The Examined Life in 2012, and for his poem. "Birds," published in The Blue Hour, 2013. Grabois's novel, *Two-Headed Dog*, is available for all e-readers for 99 cents.

Marie Lascu, born in Michigan and currently residing in New York, NY. Graduated in 2012 with a Masters in Moving Image Archiving and Preservation. Has always butted heads with the words.

Amelia M. Garcia is a spoken word poet who has performed on college stages and in poetry slams throughout the Midwestern United States. Most recently she competed in the 2013 National Poetry Slam with the Lethal Poetry Slam Team out of Chicago & founded the Pax Poetry Slam in Rockford, IL. You can find her online at facebook.com/GarciaPoetry.

BIOS

Kathryn Roberts earned her BFA in Creative Writing from Goddard College, where she served as managing editor of Guideword. Her work has appeared in various online and print journals, including Pithead Chapel, Black Heart Magazine, and Slush Pile. *Companion Plants*, her debut novel, is forthcoming from Fomite Press in spring 2014. She lives in Vermont with her partner and adopted bar cats, where she writes and paints. kathrynlroberts.tumblr.com

Lydia Ford: I am 18 years old, I reside in the beautiful mountainous state of Colorado and I bleed poetry. I've written in journals and diaries for as long as I can remember but my love of poems and the recognition for the beauty of words began just a couple years ago. I have since fallen in love with metaphor and I strive to capture the enchanting and sometimes devastating. eloquentfragments.tumblr.com

My name is **Azra Tabassum** & I am a 19 year old writer living in the South of England trying to find myself through poetry and love. There is a world inside of my head that only comes to life when I am writing it and though it is half falling apart and half nonsense, it is still one of the loveliest things I've come to know. As I grow I'll take tape and staples and put it all back together again.

Aleathia Drehmer is the co-editor of Regardless of Authority. Her most recent collection of poetry, "You Find Me Everywhere" is available from Propaganda Press. Aleathia spends her time stitching and weaving dreams in a small town in upstate New York. aleathiadrehmer.wordpress.com

BIOS

Joseph Farley edited Axe Factory from 1986 to 2010. His books and chapbooks include *Suckers, For the Birds, Longing for the Mother Tongue, Waltz of the Meatballs, Her Eyes,* and *Crow of Night.* His poetry and fiction has appeared recently in US 1 Worksheets, Verse Wisconsin, Boston Poetry Review, Wilderness House, Camel Saloon, Danse Macabre, Concrete Meat Sheet, and many other places.

T.M. Göttl is a poet, chicken snuggler, and activist living in Northeast Ohio. Her poems have appeared in many online and print publications, as well as in two chapbooks—*A Hurricane of Moths* and *Angels and Copper*—and her full-length collection, *Stretching the Window.* In 2013, she won poetry awards from the Cleveland Museum of Art and the City of Ventura, CA. Someday, she will complete the projects that she starts.

During his undergraduate career at Westfield State University, **David Walker** worked on the campus' literary arts magazine, Persona. His work appears or is forthcoming in Mad Hatter's Review, Diversion Press, Noctua Review, Paper Nautilus, and others. As a graduate student, he worked as a Teaching Assistant in two creative writing classes and is currently an adjunct instructor at three colleges.

Billi MacTighe is a poet from Eastern Massachusetts who studied English at Westfield State University. She has had poems published in Prairie Margins, Paper Nautilus, Rock&Sling, and Cease, Cows. Billi's work is centered around her personal experiences, interpreting events through her Borderline Personality Disorder: a lens that allows her to see the real and imaginary parts of life simultaneously.

BIOS

Danielle Donaldson writes from Southern California. Her work can be found in Scissors & Spackle, Welter and others.

Scherezade Siobhan is a Jungian gypsy of Indian/Catalan/ Afghan origins. She is a writer/poet/psychologist who is perennially immersed in fernweh. Her work has been published in Muse India, Danse Macabre, Bluestem Magazine, The Blue Fog Journal, PIX Quarterly, Whalesound, Mixed Fruit, Gutter Eloquence, Looseleaf Tea etcetra. She is also a Pushcart Prize nominee for poetry. She is currently writing her first book — "Viper Slang" and can be found at viperslang.tumblr.com

Alex Sparks : I'm a poet and documentary filmmaker traveling across America in my van named Dorris. I'm recently married to a beautiful little lady. I like hip-hop, iced tea, and vegetables. I want to make movies for awhile and then disappear on a farm. blog.alexsparks.tv

Koyna Tomar is a student of History at Lady Shri Ram College, DU. Apart from camping out in the dusty shelves of the college library, she keeps herself busy with photography and film making. Holidays would translate into Christopher Nolan, Wong Kar Wai, and healthy doses of Godard. The streets of Delhi, flea market finds, dream-catchers, tiny siblings in matching shoes of red — they all fit into recreating film in front of her eyes as she dances to the soundtracks of Pink Floyd and Adele.

Love
and
Other
Small
Wars

Donna Marie Riley

NEW RELEASES

Literary Sexts

a collection of short & sexy love poems

volume 1

EARLY 2014

www.ingramcontent.com/pod-product-compliance
Lightning Source LLC
Chambersburg PA
CBHW061355090426

42739CB00003B/36